FINANCIAL FREEDOM

FINANCIAL FREEDOM

Mastering Your Money Mindset

B. VINCENT

QuantumQuill Press

CONTENTS

CHAPTER 1

Introduction

The first and most important step towards achieving financial freedom is realization. Being honest with yourself to realize that you don't have the skills to manage your money is incredibly important. You need to come to terms with the fact that you still currently carry the daily feelings of money management that stem from the little girl who pinned her hope on external factors. For example, "if he loves me enough to give me money, I am then worthy enough." You hold the belief linked to that little girl within you, who believes that you are not worthy enough to manage the money that passes through your hands or to have enough money to keep yourself financially stable. Understanding with awareness where these negative thoughts stem from is also incredibly important to understand and eventually release. "What you are feeling around money is energy, either stuck or flowing." The trick is to release the trapped energy and allow it to flow.

Without mastering your money mindset, it is virtually impossible to achieve financial freedom. Many have the false belief that having lots of money allows you to live a life on your terms, but the fact is true financial freedom lies in learning how to master your financial responsibilities and what it means to you on a deep spiritual level, which is personal to you and your values. This is where true peace and a sense of control is achieved within your life. Finance is a deeply personal and spiritual subject; for many, it goes to the core of the person that they are, their self-worth, their self-respect, their self-reliance, and their identity. Therefore, the feelings that people have attached to money run deep. Financial freedom is a state of mind and is achieved by mastering your money mindset. Here's to peace and prosperity.

CHAPTER 2

Understanding Your Money Mindset

This book asks you to look inside and think deeply about your financial history, experiences, and beliefs before starting with changes or commitment to setting new money goals. You will need to understand yourself first in order to move forward and evaluate where you are going from here. You can plan as much as you like, but include what works best for you and your family. There are universal guidelines recommended by professionals and experts, but your life reality is what we will consider first. List and record your preferences, lifestyle, beliefs, and how those align with best practices when it comes to money principles, savings, goal setting, family commitments/run, income, and debt management. As you well know, you are who you are. Understanding your mental financial approach might help you get some perspective when you consider new recommendations for your financial future. Be flexible in your approach but also learn to adapt smartly the concepts given here to your life.

The way we view our finances, think about money, act in relation to money, and relate to others around money is what contributes to our unique personal money mindset. Everyone's relationship with money is unique, as it is based on a combination of factors including our upbringing, experiences, emotions, and actions. Our money mindset influences everything about us - choices, decisions, and ambitions. So, what is your personal approach to managing financial decisions and planning your future? The first steps in understanding your money mindset include identifying your personal beliefs and attitudes towards money. Consider the following questions. Also, look at other people you know and respect around you and how they treat money, what values do they hold for its purpose.

2.1. Identifying Limiting Beliefs

Beliefs act as barriers that limit our potential, keeping us stuck and blocking us from thinking and feeling differently about the life that we crave. When we believe something to be true, we search for evidence that will validate our belief. Those things we believe to be true will inevitably come to our awareness because we are searching for proof of our beliefs. When our searches confirm our belief, it becomes even stronger. Methodologically, beliefs are the reason we procrastinate. We state, "I believe I'm going to fail," "I believe I'm too fat to wear this," "I believe I won't be successful in that job," etc. And because of these beliefs, we intentionally or unintentionally commit acts of self-sabotage. It's not our behavior that determines our outcome; it's our beliefs. The benefits we gain from our beliefs act as a deterrent, keeping us from letting go of them.

Beliefs stand in the way of our financial success. Our beliefs are habitual thoughts that we think over and over again, and with consistency, we develop entire belief systems. Contrary to popular belief, we are not our beliefs. Our beliefs aren't a part of our identity, but they are like a lens that shapes the way we see ourselves and the world around us. By changing your beliefs, you change your perspective, and your perception changes. It's like witnessing a miracle.

Beliefs also serve as a mental shortcut because they allow us to make predictions about future events. Any experience we encounter that doesn't fit within the boundaries of our beliefs is dismissed as insignificant and ignored. As a result, we can miss out on positive experiences and opportunities because they don't make sense through the lens of our beliefs.

2.2. Overcoming Fear and Scarcity Mentality

Scarcity Mentality: In our society, most of us are motivated by the drive for power, fame, and learning the language of money to survive in our environment. Scarcity mentality at this point is heightened and we all start to place our minds into a negative spiral, where we avoid risk, making decisions, being a leader, etc. has given some things that will prevent one from achieving their potential. Some of the repercussions of Scarcity Mentality are: 1. We unknowingly assume that others' success comes at the cost of our own chance to succeed. 2. We see others as competition and constantly compare ourselves to them. 3. We find ourselves caught in endless cycles of jealousy and resentment. 4. Our low self-esteem inhibits our creative abilities, forcing us to compare ourselves with other high achievers.

2.2. Overcoming Fear and Scarcity Mentality: Fear in itself is a big roadblock to achieving our potential. Financial fear inhibits us from making reasonable decisions, being too cautious, or taking wild chances. Working towards finding a way to overcome this fear is necessary for us to take calculated risks such as changing employers, changing professions, investing in assets, etc. shows that the mind is both starved for certainty and afraid of uncertainty. This fear of uncertainty restricts our movements and abilities to become aware and act on what is at the root of fear. Basically, we fear the unknown, what we don't know and can't predict are all the possible outcomes of a particular situation ranging from devastating to mildly inconvenient, which in turn prevents us from venturing out beyond our current state. gave some ways to mitigate the tendency to become overly anxious when confronted with ambiguous situations.

2.3. Cultivating a Growth Mindset

Author and peak performance expert Stephen Covey found that people with the following characteristics are more successful: goal-oriented, seeking continual improvement, curious, inspired by entrepreneurship, appreciative of growth, trainable, productive, innovative, adaptable, and managers of conflicts. With a growth mindset, when we take entrepreneurial action through moving towards our goals, even if we make a "mistake" or enroll in the University of Adversity, we understand it's just part of the process. We look for the lesson and redefine our line toward success. Do you have a growth mindset? Do you feel you are growing vs. feeling stagnant in your business and life? How are you viewing your adversity episodes/non-mistakes? Are you open to feedback?

Cultivating a growth mindset. A growth mindset refers to an optimistic view of an ever-expanding future and a desire to learn, grow, and expand into the person you were meant to become. In business, career, family life, and personal relationships, growth allows you to expand your creative energy to shape and create the life you desire. Psychologist and researcher Carol Dweck from Stanford University describes a growth mindset leads to a desire to learn and recognize failures as part of the learning process. Cultivating a growth mindset will allow you to remain adaptable and continue to grow yourself and your business and provides invaluable tools for understanding where others are coming from. It also allows you to continually discover creative, adaptive solutions when dealing with life's challenges and opportunities without becoming overwhelmed or paralyzed.

CHAPTER 3

Building a Strong Financial Foundation

The same is true when it comes to financial freedom. In order to build true wealth, you must establish a strong foundation. The bigger the foundation, the more opportunity you have to spread out your risk load. For example, a true wealth building foundation would include some asset classes such as real estate investing, some traditional mutual fund, stock and options investing, and hard money lending or investing. A small foundation would include one or two of these asset classes. At the same time, though, if you are seriously religious or have religious inhibitors toward one or more of these things (i.e. options investing or hard money lending), don't do it. You should invest in things that keep you comfortable about the amount you are investing and that do not violate your core values.

Nothing is more important than establishing a strong foundation. Building a house is a perfect example. Before you start the framing of a house, you have to have a good foundation on which to build your house. A house's foundation is typically made of concrete and encompasses the entire footprint of the house. By creating a large enough footprint, you are spreading out the load of the house. This creates a strong foundation. However, if you were to try and build a house, even if it was small or contained very intricate framing, on a small foundation or all rock foundation, the house will eventually settle, causing problems in the framing, walls, and service lines.

3.1. Setting Financial Goals

Setting financial goals will require time and deep thought. You will need to assess your finances and determine short-term income goals, medium-term income goals, and long-term income goals. In life, some elements of time and money are non-negotiable, such as tax or time as an asset. But here is the thing: work must be completed to make money, debts must be settled, taxes must be paid. Although time is not negotiable, the way we spend our time is under our control. So, at times, the most valuable non-negotiable items like time, taxes, and non-investment money need to be managed. And then it would help if you set financial goals.

Setting financial goals is important for reaching them. Having goals encourages you to plan, think about what you want, and move toward your dreams. By setting specific financial goals, you're able to break the journey to financial freedom into smaller, more manageable tasks, each with a deadline and methods of accountability. You are also able to quantify how much savings you need to accumulate or which debt you should pay first. This, in turn, motivates you to alter your spending habits in ways that will enable you to live within your means and prioritize spending that is aligned with your financial goals.

3.2. Creating a Budget

Determining your expenses is another important consideration for budgeting. This will help you see how much money you spend each month. When you track your expenses, make sure to include everything. The goal is to have clarity with your expenses. This way you can see the actual number in relation to what you can afford. Expenses fall into three categories: fixed expenses, variable expenses, and discretionary expenses. Fixed expenses are essential bills or expenses that do not change or change very little each month. Variable expenses, this category is divided into four groups: needs, wants, utilities, and non-budgeted items. Discretionary expenses are non-essential items that are optional; they fall under several categories. One of the biggest reasons budgets fail is that they are inflexible. Quirks like gas prices, children's growth, inflation, birthdays, etc., can cause your budget to buckle under the pressure.

Creating a budget is crucial in managing your money wisely. Without a budget, you don't have a clear understanding of where your money's going. This can lead to confusion and even piling debt. When creating a budget, you'll need to understand how much money you have and determine where it needs to go. This is going to give you a clear view of what you're spending on and how long it's going to last. The four steps to create the budget are as follows: determine your income, calculate living expenses, plan for net and spending, and analyze and adjust your budget.

3.3. Managing Debt Effectively

Perhaps you and your friend both have some money in your budget and agree to go on a $300 each camping trip. If your friend comes back and has saved up $300, and you have saved up $400 for the camping trip, you have matched your friend's saved amount.

Remember, affordability has to do with supply and demand. If you reduce supply, you can afford more. If you increase demand, you can afford less. Substitution is a method of reducing demand. Instead of going on an expensive spring break trip with friends, you could take a low-cost camping trip. For example, Challenge Yourself to Save is a campaign that encourages people to save for a year and to save as much as reasonable. If you take a camping trip and save the money that you would have spent on a more expensive trip, you can put that $400 into the pot.

Next, look at all of your purchases and their costs — from your house payment and car insurance to grabbing a candy bar from the vending machine at work or eating out a few times each week. It all adds up. Determine the amount that you need to spend to have your monthly spending match your budget. The rest can go towards your debt.

What do you do after you have evaluated your debt and determined a plan to pay it off? The next step is to create a plan and a budget. It is important to find out where your spending has to fall in order for you to pay off your highest priority debt before your grace period ends. Decide how much you will need to pay towards that debt with each paycheck and how much you can afford to spend in order to have funds available to pay that amount. Adjust necessary expenses to ensure that your funds are there.

3.4. Saving and Investing

There's an obvious disconnect here: putting money aside is essential – it's one of the main actions that will lead to your financial goals. However, this is about doing it in a positive way. A woman who is able to replace "stop spending" with "start having extra money" has already taken a major step towards seeing her financial goals met. So, stop assuming that "spending less and less" is synonymous with being able to save and replace that mindset with "as of today, I am able to start having extra money". That positive attitude will lead to a higher paying job, making some extra cash in your after-hours, and having work and vacation bonuses, and not just saving the money you manage to cut from spending.

You've become an expert in tracking your spending, you think about your financial goals now in terms of actual numbers, and you're able to comfortably discuss and write down your financial goals. Now let's work on how to actually achieve those goals. Make no mistake: saving and investing are crucial for achieving major financial goals. Where will you get the money from, otherwise? Here's the thing: in Cuba, saving is synonymous with putting money aside, which is another word for spending less. Many personal finance blogs have a different take on this: they believe that this concept is too negative, and most people don't get excited about spending less and less. That's why it's better to tell them they should "work on having extra money to spend".

CHAPTER 4

Mastering Money Habits
for Financial Freedom

2. When we think, feel, and believe we are not financially free, we make decisions from that belief and become even less financially free. How do we create our mindset completely centered on an infinite path for wealth and abundance? A Money Mindset approaches wealth as something that doesn't exist 'out there'. It exists in the minds of successful people. A Money Mindset approach is personally tailored with a plan, strategizing every day, while it's based on three simple successes: The power of belief, which is your intellectual and faith-based blueprint focusing on your wealth. While you work and think alongside the blueprint, acting forward even when things go differently than envisioned. The love of wealth begins with respect for a dollar. Research the right money habits to respect the disciplines that successful investors have put into practice. Reading about people's financial achievements and powers, like Warren Buffet or Oprah Winfrey, must impact your passion. Treasuring wealth is how you feel every time you balance a bank statement. You should feel the dedication in mind, body, and spirit."

1. "Money habits are our thoughts and beliefs around money. They guide the way we choose to manage our finances. Mastering money habits can lead to financial freedom. How can we master our money habits for financial freedom? By changing our money mindset. The money mindset is our attitude and overall understanding of wealth and finances. To reach financial freedom, we must keep habits that lead in the direction of wealth. Yet, the truth of the matter is, most of us have money habits leading us in an opposite direction. We all make money decisions based on emotional responses, stress, and expectations because we have to make these decisions every single day. It affects us greatly because we are giving money to a source external from our businesses, careers, and passion to sustain our everyday living.

4.1. Developing Smart Spending Habits

Children in the pre-operational (age 2-7) and concrete operational stages (age 7-12) in Piaget's cognitive development model are limited by their immature reasoning skills. For example, during the preoperational stage, children's thinking is influenced by immediate appearance. Children in this stage may not understand that a $20 check can be exchanged for two $10 bills, because obviously, two simply looks like a larger number than one. During the period of the concrete operational stage, children's understanding of conservation, which involves the ability to understand that changing the shape of an object does not change the amount, has been well-documented. They understand that half a pizza is the same amount of pizza as half of a pizza. Children's understanding of conservation is a precursor to understanding of more simple financial concepts, such as reinvesting dividends and the time value of money, and investing to benefit from compound interest. To help our students get a head start on learning about investing, we need to understand where their cognitive development and life experience have arisen up to that point to address any misconceptions.

In the current climate of instant gratification and consumerism, teaching smart spending habits can be very challenging. However, financial literacy education has to include money management skills, such as budgeting and saving. An important part of learning about money is understanding that we have multiple wants and limited resources. We can have a new toy now, but it will mean giving up on an outing to the zoo next week. The ability to make decisions about how we want to spend our funds, weighing our priorities in the process, is a fundamental life skill. Children who do not learn about cost-benefit analyses in play and saving for a rainy day will be at a disadvantage when they need to make far more important financial decisions later on.

4.2. Automating Finances for Success

This is the best option to ensure a fully balanced budget is paid (after one has been created). It is also a foolproof way to make sure that you are setting money aside for those irregular bills. Saving some of your "mad money" for a larger, more fulfilling purchase later on, rather than wasting it on whatever strikes your fancy first. Many people say that automation caused them to overspend. Studies show the opposite! Automation does not lead to overspending, it leads to freedom because it automates savings. It's like "out of sight, out of mind", and before you know it, you'll have that 5% raise fully automated into the account by December. A lot of studies show that people attempt living below their means (many say by at least 10%) in an attempt to pay off debt, build wealth, or to avoid debt altogether. Done correctly, this is a source of financial freedom. What if someone does not succeed in avoiding overspending or buying things uncautiously? Wouldn't that be a debt avoidance/wealth-building source of financial stress?

So many people want to know where their money goes every month and are either too lazy to figure out a budget or think a budget is too hard. Until the recent boom in personal finance apps, the only other financial option was to make multiple transfers to different accounts per paycheck. One went to the bank, the other to a "house" fund, and another went to a savings account for non-monthly bills. A money magician to shuffle all that money, it really was magic because I am far too lazy for that many steps. However, we are the rare individuals that had millionaire parents, a PhD in economics, and an introduction to the world of personal finance at 18. Of course, I majored in Business. I was taught this mindset from a young age. Not everyone is as lucky as I was, and not everyone gets the exposure I was getting to the personal finance community at such a young age.

4.3. Building Multiple Streams of Income

Another way is to set up an almost self-sufficient setup, where you have a passive income along with debt reduction. You can book a new rental property. Take a loan and start repayment immediately (even if the construction isn't complete). By the time the property is complete, you would have made a substantial down payment. Check whether the same is tax-deductible. Once the rental income starts, it should cover the bank EMI, not necessarily from a market perspective. It would be ratio-based. As time passes (typically 10-15 years), you eventually generate a massive rental income, which directly benefits you and also the EMI on the loan. This creates an extremely positive income. Debts start reducing as and when the rental yield increases. As a corollary, you have a property asset which would have appreciated over time.

Now that we know what passive income is, we need to think of ways to receive this type of income. One way is through investing. In the Indian context, two things help in receiving the benefits of passive income through investment. The first is compound interest, and the second is tax benefits. With investments such as mutual funds, equity shares, and bonds, you can earn compound interest or reinvest your earnings. By doing so, you can receive the benefits of compounded interest, which means that the longer the money stays invested, the greater the benefit thanks to compounded interest.

4.4. Protecting Your Financial Future

While we must accept responsibility for acting on knowledge, there's something else that makes people prosperous in life. That's the key to truly empowering your finances. It's about persistently being disciplined as you spend money and setting aside money in emergency and retirement funds. It decides how much you could do toward growing your wealth. Attend to it. Read the handout every day. The greater exposure, the stronger it will get. Operating legend has it that after he became famous, Paul Newman was once asked by an interviewer about the amount of acting he had done before. Newman picked up a phone, referred to the number in his Palm Pilot, quietly said, "How much?" then swooped an eyebrow up at the stranger and remarked, "Talent helps too, you know." Now, why in the world would you look at a blank entry where talent should be, and a $3.10 worth of potential savings, when you could be improving those numbers to a $3.50 or more each day?

At this point, you have gained quite a bit of knowledge in various areas to help you on your way to financial discipline and general fiscal responsibility. You might be inundated by debt with collection agencies hot on your trail yet. Or, through long-time neglect of your checking account, you may be stuck with a negative balance in the resource. As such, implementing the techniques I've been talking about is easier if you start being proactive with your money, rather than reacting to what happened previously. Yet you simply have to, because it's the only way to eventually overcome your financial problems and become secure. If you read the title of this course you probably have seemingly unrealistic goals in mind right now too. Here's your opportunity to reduce your cynicism. I guarantee that the time and energy you put into creating a viable budget, setting aside funds for emergencies and retirement, learning to make money work for you, and turning from the biggest and most effective consumer to the most productive saver, will make all the difference.

As you focus on the different areas of your financial situation, it's easy to get bogged down and want to quit. Financial planning can become daunting if you allow it to become that way. Refrain from allowing your financial situation in its entirety to get the best of you. Let's look at some ways to simplify the entire process and keep it from overwhelming you.

Milton Keynes UK
Ingram Content Group UK Ltd.
UKHW031207251124
451566UK00010B/189